# YOU FUCKING C

# SCORPIO

# SCORPIO

## OCTOBER 23RD — NOVEMBER 21ST

### MARS & PLUTO

DETERMINED BRAVE
LOYAL HONEST
AMBITIOUS SECRETIVE
STUBBORN
ENTICING
DEEPLY COMPASSIONATE
HONEST ASSERTIVE
SMART
STOIC SENSITIVE
MOODY AMBITIOUS
DIRECT

ALIGNMENT CRYSTALS

WHITE TOPAZ
LAPIS LAZULI
BLOODSTONE
DIAMOND
RUBY
MALACHITE SUNSTONE
CLEAR QUARTZ
RED JASPER
TURQUISE

# YOU MATTER

ENJOY

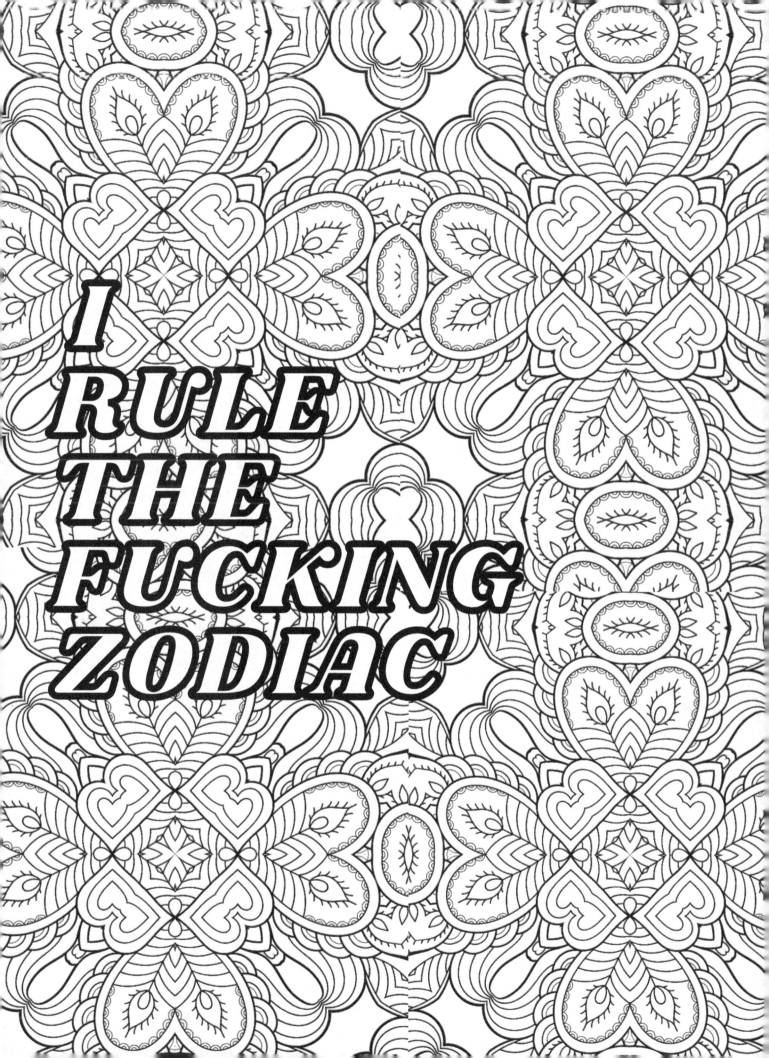

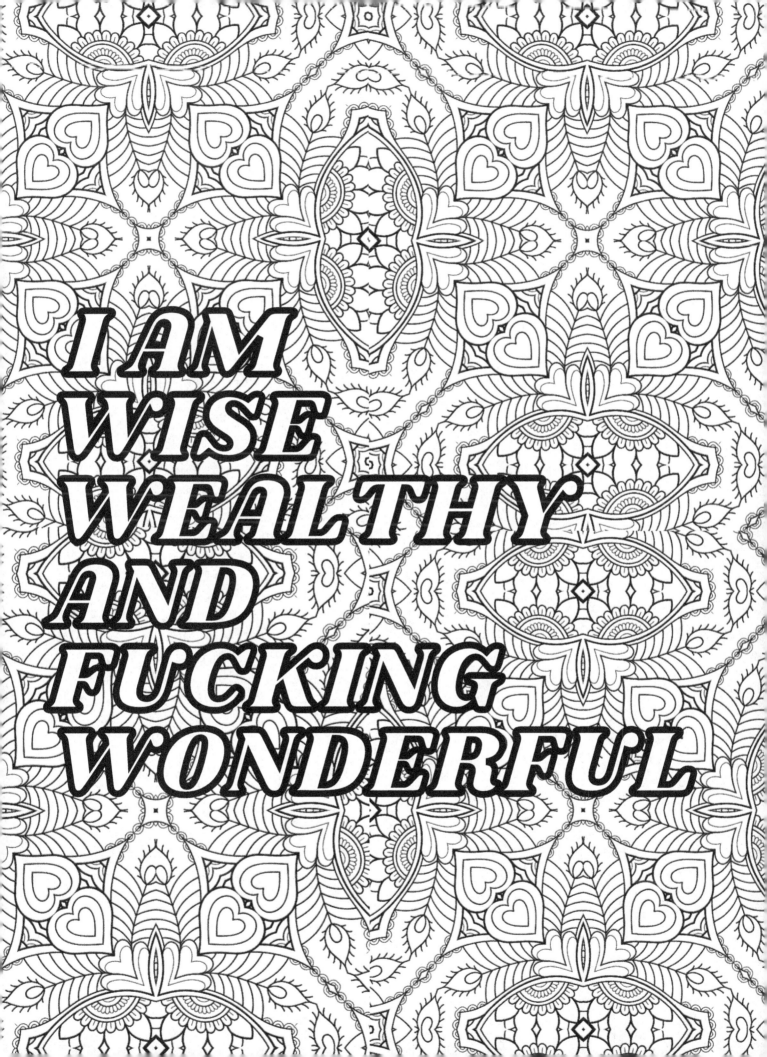

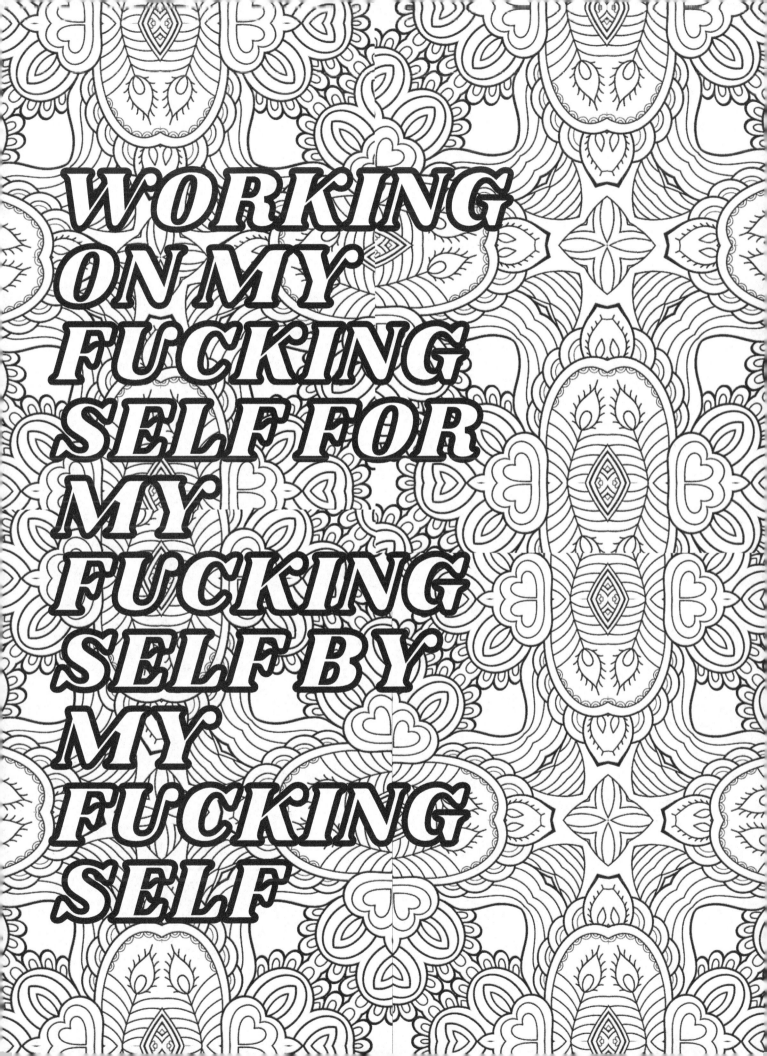

SOMETIMES THE ONE WHO SITS ON THE THRONE IS A FUCKING SCORPIO

AN SCORPIO BELIEVED THEY COULD SO THEY DID

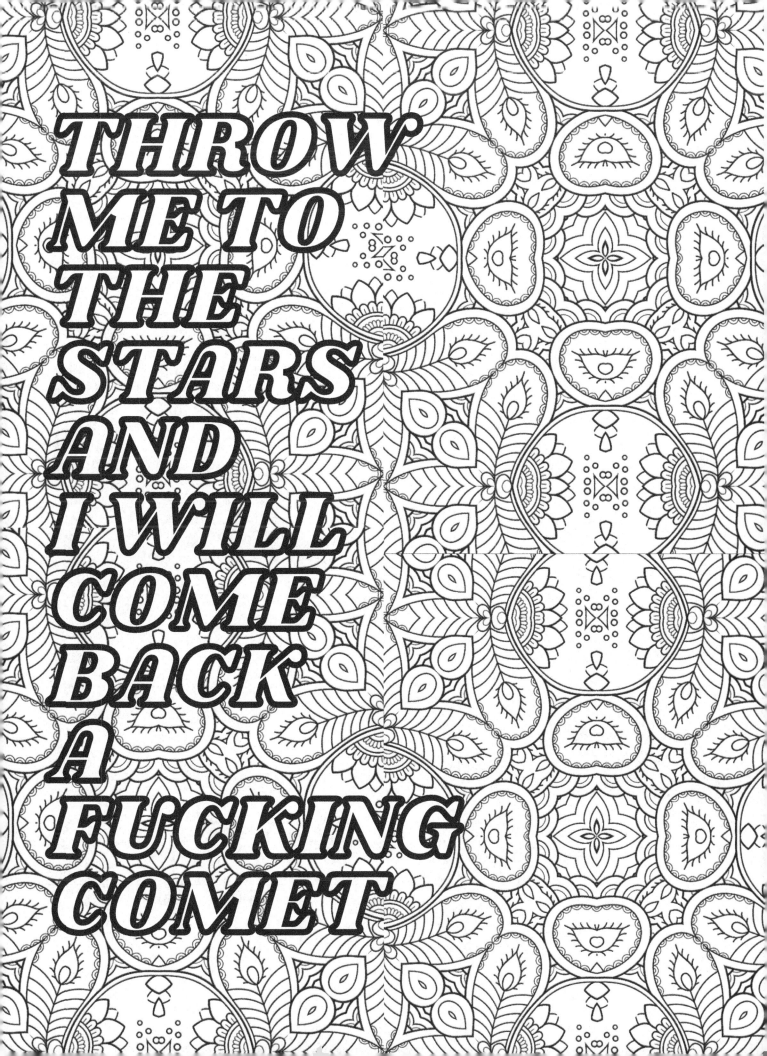

EMPOWERED SCORPIO EMPOWER THE HELL OUT OF THE FUCKING ZODIAC

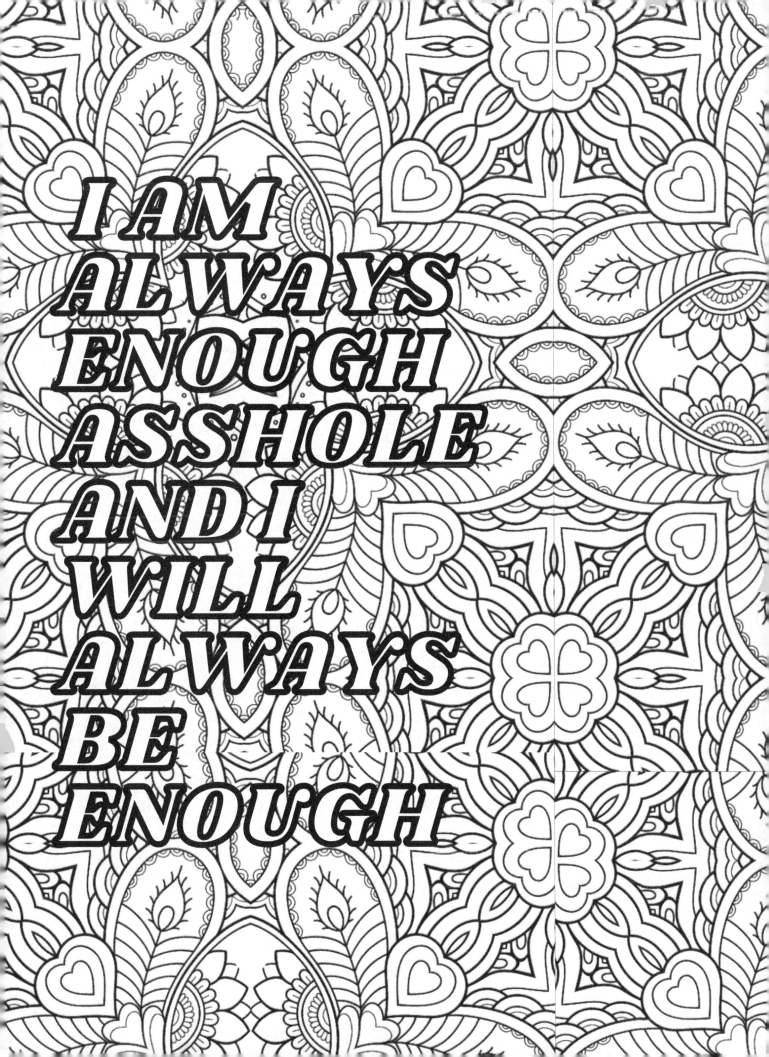

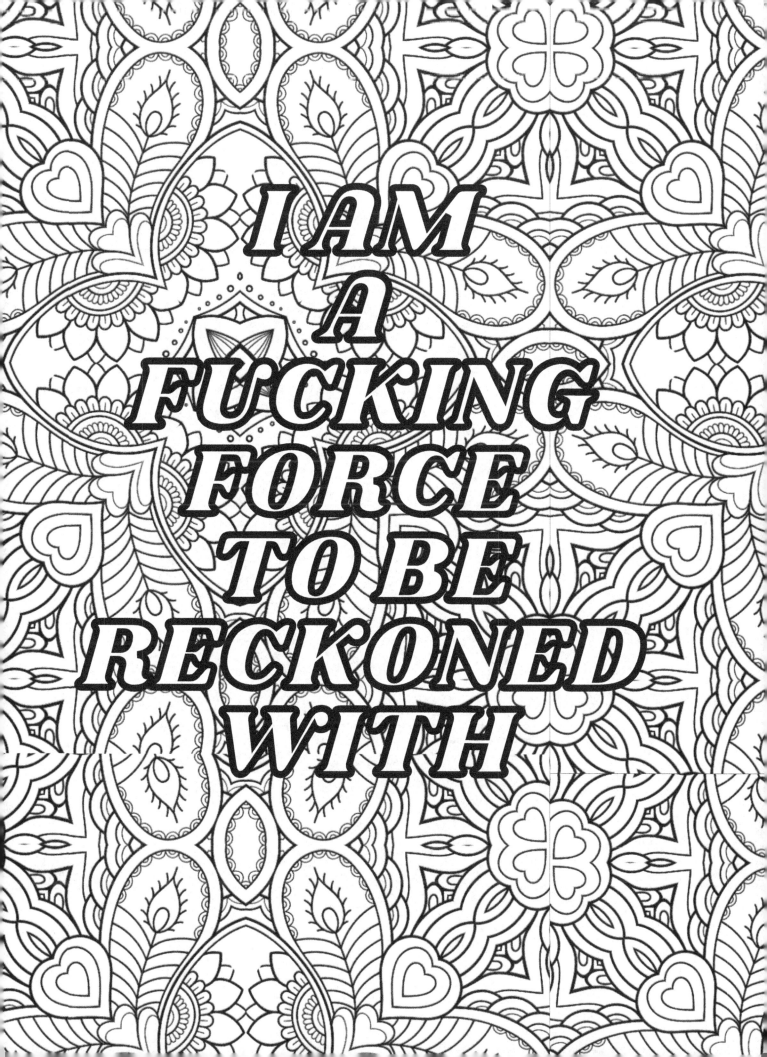

IN A WORLD FULL OF CHOICES

THANK YOU FOR

CHOOSING US

Made in the USA
Las Vegas, NV
06 December 2024